VIEWS FROM THE CROSS

VIEWS FROM THE CROSS

Conversations with Jesus on Calvary

Denise J. Brennan

Illustrations by Julie Lonneman

For information regarding permissions, write to:
A Cappela Publishing
P. O. Box 3691
Sarasota FL 34230-3691

LIBRARY OF CONGRESS CATALOGING-IN-PUBLICATION DATA
Brennan, Denise J.
Views from the Cross / Denise J. Brennan
p. cm.
ISBN 978-0-9818933-5-8
1. Religion 2. Philosophy 3. Christ I. Title

Book design by Carol Tornatore

First Edition

Printed in Canada

Acknowledgments

Dedicated in everlasting gratitude to my parents:
Senator Joseph Brennan and Ita Ryan Brennan

I EXTEND SINCERE appreciation to Donia and Anraí ó Braonáin of Baile Átha Cliath in Ireland. Without their encouragement this book would not have been written. Katherine Skelly gave me her constant help. Early in the process of preparing the text for publication, Bernardine Dawes' expertise was invaluable. Carolyn J Lewis, a superb book editor, worked with me over a long period of time. Penelope Dugan graciously brought Carolyn to my attention. Others, who greatly assisted me, include Lloyd J Thomas Ph.D., Jack Pudney, Rev. Frank Muscolino, Rev. John Waldron, Sister Margaret MacCurtain O.P., Rev Frank Doyle SJ, Maureen Murphy, Rev John Malecki Ph.D. and Marilyn Gustin Ph.D.

I am most grateful to Patrika Vaughn and the staff of A Cappela Publishing. Carol Tornatore brought her great skills to the final design of this book. Julie Lonneman's woodcut illustrations have greatly enhanced the text.

The presence of friends and family has been a daily blessing for me. I sincerely thank all of them for their support and encouragement.

Contents

Introduction

PEOPLE TALK TO each other and share whatever is on their minds.

Jesus is no exception.

Since returning to full human life on the first Easter Day, he has enjoyed conversing with his friends.

No one enjoys a good chat more than he does.

His view of our human experience has not changed since Calvary. He shares this view from the Cross with his Father. They continually, *with divine gentleness*, invite us to welcome their Spirit of love into our bodies, minds and souls. They invite us to Heaven. This is Heaven: sharing their *and our Views from the Cross.*

Prologue

JESUS DIED, BUT he overcame death. By the time he died, there was nothing to hold him back from life. He was totally free. He emptied himself from any possibility of self-limiting possessiveness. And so he rose to indestructible life.

Jesus is alive. He invites us to share a view. This is the same view that he enjoyed—yes!—enjoyed from his standpoint on Calvary. He wants us to see what he, our risen friend, saw from the Cross. Each person's experience, looking from Calvary with Jesus, brings a new perspective to that view. Jesus, alive and well, invites us to talk to him, to his family, to his friends and among ourselves so as to share our insights from the hill that overlooks, not only Jerusalem, but the whole world. We benefit from listening in to the conversations that Jesus continues to have with his friends who have died and now share with Jesus his view from the Cross. Jesus' original perspective from Calvary, on the first Good Friday, was agonizingly clear. He was not encumbered by any distracting consolation. His pain only allowed him to experience love. He looked out with an unobstructed view of pure love. He hasn't changed his view. He still looks out over each of us with the same unalterable divine love.

Looking out from Calvary, Jesus continues to have the same intense desire in his heart that we would be able to become all that we would like to be. He knows that obstacles can get in our way, hindering us from becoming fully and completely the unique person each one of us was created to be. So, the first topic of conversation Jesus and his friends engage in is *the ability to see without distortion—in a word CLARITY*.

VIEWS FROM THE CROSS

Jesus of Nazareth

1

Clarity

ST. PAUL is known as the "Apostle to the Gentiles. In the Book of Acts, his conversion is described as he was traveling on the road to Damascus. He was thrown to the ground and he heard the voice of Jesus calling him to bring the good news of salvation to people throughout the Roman Empire.

Jesus chose PETER as the leader of his Apostles. He was a fisherman from Galilee. It is believed that it was when Nero was Emperor of Rome that Peter died a martyr about the year 64 AD.

A FRIEND OF Jesus, Paul of Tarsus, looked out from Calvary. He asked Jesus, "Lord how did you end up here?"

Jesus answered, "It was uphill for me, Paul; all the way to here from Bethlehem and Nazareth. Throughout my life since childhood, my outlook and attitude were constantly widening until I reached this unobstructed view from Calvary. Paul, I believe you of all people, appreciate the experience of one's view of life expanding. I'm thinking of how you looked at things differently after you were knocked to the ground."

Paul saw that Jesus had a broad smile on his face.

"It wasn't so funny Lord, at the time, I can tell you. But, you are right. People can read about my experience in Luke's *Acts of the Apostles*. It dramatically changed my view. I now know that you jolted me into sharing your view from your Cross."

Jesus turned to some visitors to Calvary nearby. Among them was a group of friends including two famous writers, Hilaire Belloc and C.S. Lewis.

JOSEPH HILAIRE PIERRE RENE BELLOC (27 July, 1870 – 16 July, 1953) was a French-born writer who became a naturalized British subject in 1902. He was one of the most prolific writers in England during the early twentieth century.

CLIVE STAPLES "JACK" LEWIS (29 November, 1898 – 22 November, 1963), commonly referred to as C. S. Lewis, was an Irish writer and scholar. Lewis' works are diverse and include medieval literature, Christian apologetics, literary criticism, radio broadcasts, essays on Christianity, and fiction relating to the fight between good and evil. Examples of Lewis' allegorical fiction include *The Screwtape Letters, The Chronicles of Narnia* and *The Space Trilogy.*

He reminded them what had happened to Paul. "Paul's conversion is described in Acts 9: 1–20. He falls to the ground, as a result of a flash of light from the sky, as he hears the words 'Saul, Saul why are you persecuting me?' That was me, of course, speaking."

"Yes, Lord you certainly knocked me off my high horse! I myself described this conversion experience in Acts 22: 1–22 and in Acts 26: 1–24. I, blinded by the light, was led to Damascus in Syria where I was baptized. Up to that time, I had been blinded by my prejudices as a Pharisee. I needed that jolt you gave me Lord. It opened my mind. I was able to take in your expansive vision of love. I *see* now that everything you did and said in your public ministry indicated that you wanted to achieve an unstoppable advance to Calvary. You came there to share with all of us the universal, authentic *and clear* panorama of the human family."

"Yes Paul. From Calvary, *I saw and continue to see* every person and every situation." My view *from* the Cross which I want to share with everyone was *and still* is comprehensive, just as the psalmist says in Psalm 33:

From the place where he dwells he gazes
On all the dwellers on the earth
He who shapes the hearts of all
And considers all their deeds."

Then Jesus turned to Katharine Drexel, who devoted her life to education, and invited her to share her thoughts.

KATHARINE MARY DREXEL (November 26, 1858 – March 3, 1955) was canonized a Saint by Pope John Paul II on October 1, 2000. She was the daughter of Philadelphia banker Francis Anthony Drexel. On 12 February, 1891, Katharine founded the Sisters of the Blessed Sacrament in order to provide schools for Native Americans and African Americans. She dedicated her life and personal fortune of US $20 million to this work.

She answered, "Lord, as I listen to you and Paul talking I am reminded that your vision from the Cross comes from the agony of love that immolated your humanity. I hope that my ministry of education helped people to see themselves and others with *the clarity* of your view. It is so *clear* from the Cross. There is no distortion from greed. There is no selfish mist clouding one's vision."

One of the writers, C. S. Lewis, spoke: "Yes, Katharine, when the clarity of seeing our-selves and others from the Cross is lost, we lose Jesus' undivided vision of love. We use tags like 'moderate' and 'extreme' or 'liberal' and 'conservative.' One result, from looking out from Calvary over Jerusalem and beyond to the world, is that all of those labels are *dropped*."

"Really, Lewis?" asked Hilaire Belloc.

Lewis answered: "That's right. Once you start looking out from here, all the labels are dropped into the waste basket. The only tag or classification needed is *human*. The view from the Cross *clearly* sees through all the divisive labels. There are no liberals, no conservatives, no far right, no far left — just people.

Paul nodded: "Yes, Lewis, with Jesus we see people *clearly*. Then he turned to Jesus: "Lord, I came to understand that everyone gets a *clear* view of the human family from Calvary. Standing here next to you I'm beginning to understand that this is indeed a view free from distortion, the fruit of which is unlimited and universal love."

"You're right about that, Paul," Jesus said. This gives you an indication of the *love born from the clarity of seeing out from the Cross."*

Paul nodded his head and realized that this involved Jesus having to travel in time and space into the tunnel of death, from which he would emerge complete.

Paul smiled and said with a broad grin, "Lord, *I see clearly now:* that's your goal, isn't it? The *completion* of each human being."

2

Completion

JESUS CONTINUED HIS conversation with Paul. "If you look out with me from Calvary you'll be able to see clearly that my Father simply wants us to reach our complete authentic selves. The longer you look out with me from this hill, the better you'll understand that to be saved simply means to be truly oneself. When the structure of human society enables us to become completely and authentically the special persons we were created to be, I will know that my work of salvation has reached completion."

These words of Jesus confirmed for Paul that God's desire was that all children would reach their full humanity. Paul remembered that Jesus said to the man dying beside him on another cross: "This day you will be with me in Paradise." Paul understood that what Jesus meant by *paradise* was the happy ending of the journey to reach the fullness of our humanity.

Paul said: "Lord, your words are amazing. In the midst of your experience of total pain envelopment and the absence of even one single nerve ending of solace, you invited a companion in agony, to leave space and time and come to completion."

"You must understand, Paul," Jesus said, "that I was driven inwardly to fulfillment and resurrection. Surely that's clear. I had often spoken to your friend Peter and my other companions, about having to go to Jerusalem. This was the city from where I would take the final journey to completion."

Paul smiled and said, "Lord, that's your goal isn't it—that each person realizes her or his humanity?"

"Exactly," Jesus said. "That is why I earnestly encourage everyone to appreciate all the sciences, all the arts and letters. These pursuits are crucial in helping each person reach her or his completion."

Paul continued looking from Calvary with Jesus, while remaining silent. He was thinking of his mission in life. He traveled from city to city, inviting people to share Jesus' vision from the Cross. Paul wanted people to be grateful for knowing what Jesus wants for us. He wants our human completion. He wants this for the Chinese students locked up and forgotten. He wants, Jesus wants, the little Afghan girl to reach her own unique fullness. Paul agreed with the Cistercian monk and writer, Thomas Merton, who recognized our common experience of "incompleteness."

THOMAS MERTON (January 31, 1915 – December 10, 1968) was a Trappist monk and one of the most influential Catholic authors of the 20th century.

In order to heal our pain of feeling unfulfilled, Paul remembered that Jesus told us that he had come on earth so that we would "have life and have it more abundantly." He was aware from sharing his Lord's view from the Cross, that Jesus had come to make it possible for each person to attain completeness.

"Lord Jesus," Paul said, "your priesthood, your mission is our completion. That's your *vocation.*"

Jesus smiled.

3

Vocation

Mary of Nazareth

T WAS ANOTHER pleasant afternoon on the hill overlooking Jerusalem. Another group of friends had come together.

Jesus was talking. "That was my vocation: to be myself. The titles people give me — Priest, King, Savior, Lord, Messiah, Anointed One, Son of David describe all that I did to fulfill this vocation to be myself. Our identity comes from being *who* we are. God reveals God by saying 'I am who am.' Each of us can say, 'I am.' Our *being* is our identity — our being the *fully* human person we are — that is our vocation."

Jesus' mother, Mary, spoke. "It's not just that Jesus became human; it's his embrace of the human experience of each of us that is mind-boggling. He has pulled into his own heart the sum-total experience of joy, suffering, hopes and dreams of every person that has lived or ever will live. He joins with them in their quest to become fully human, fully themselves. While physicists continue to learn about the pull of gravity and other forces in our universe, Jesus teaches us about another gravitational pull, the magnetic power that our humanity has on God."

Mary's husband Joseph was the next to speak.

"There is hope. Millions of people are sharing with Jesus the vocation to be human and fulfilling their calling very well. There are attorneys, doctors, artists, bus drivers, nuns, bank managers, dairy farmers, writers, laundry workers, booksellers, welders, composers, monks and electricians. They

JOSEPH OF NAZARETH

are the answer to the petition: 'Let us pray for vocations.'"

Elizabeth of Hungary spoke.

"For Jesus, that means, "Let us pray to be human. Let us pray to be simply ourselves and assist others to be themselves. We rejoice as we look out

ELIZABETH (1207-1231) was the daughter of King Andrew II of Hungary. Elizabeth was married at the age of fourteen. Her husband died when she was twenty. She used all her wealth to help the poor. She became a symbol of Christian charity after her death at the age of twenty four.

from the Cross. We see the artists Rembrandt van Rijn and Mary Cassatt, the scientists Albert Einstein and Marie Curie, the statesmen Mahatma Gandhi and Anwar Sadat. We are thrilled that all of them fulfilled their first and supreme vocation to be *human*, to be fully themselves."

The group of friends that had gathered that afternoon on Calvary included the Irish monk, Dom Columba Marmion.

Everyone looked forward to hearing what this great teacher had to say. They had read all his books. He spoke. "The process of people becoming themselves began evolving thousands of years, before the process of becoming Zen, Christian, Muslim, or Agnostic. Look out from this hill called Calvary with God and know it's *about being human.*"

Dom Marmion smiled. "Jesus didn't become Irish. Jesus did *not* become Catholic. Jesus did *not* become Orthodox. Jesus did *not* become Protestant. Jesus did *not* become Hindu. He never changed his religion. He became human. That's all he did. He took humanity into his being. By the time he rose,

DOM COLUMBA MARMION (April 1, 1858 – January 30, 1923) He was a priest in Dublin, Ireland, before becoming a Benedictine monk. He was Abbot of Maredsous Abbey in Belgium. His spiritual books have been translated into many languages. He was beatified by Pope John Paul II on September 3, 2000.

he had, through childhood, adolescence and adulthood, in joy and great pain, *become completely human*. He fulfilled his *vocation*. Alleluia!"

Dom Marmion stood up and reverently lifted his arm towards a group of Jesus' apostles sitting close by; Andrew, James and John, Nathaniel and some others. "None of these men changed their religion. What they did was to fulfill their *vocation* to become *fully human, fully themselves*."

4

Fully Human Fully Ourselves

JESUS LOOKED OUT across human history from Calvary. He turned to see who was approaching to share the view with him. It was a man whose books Jesus knew had helped a great number of people, Father Anthony de Mello, a Jesuit priest from India.

"Come and sit with me Tony," Jesus said as he stretched out his hand to his friend.

"Thank you Lord. You know as I was coming up the hill to join you, your Holy Spirit got me to thinking about William Shakespeare's *Hamlet*."

"Oh yes, Tony, I wonder why?" Jesus asked.

"Well Lord, I believe your Spirit feels that Shakespeare teaches us a profound truth in the conversation that Polonius, the counselor to the king of Denmark, had with his son Laertes. I

ANTHONY DE MELLO (1931-1987) was a Jesuit priest. He was a spiritual writer whose influence is still very strong throughout the world.

remembered that early in the play, Laertes is departing from the palace at Elsinore to return to France. Before he departs, his father speaks to him.

'This above all, to thine own self be true,
And it must follow, as the night the day,
Thou canst not then be false to any man.'"

Jesus interrupted his friend. "Indeed! Tony, this is wonderful advice. It expresses what I wanted to pass on from my Father. That's why we sent the Holy Spirit; to get people to recognize that their vocation from God, is to be *fully and truly who they are.* Each person has a calling to become herself, or himself, just as my vocation was to be fully human, fully myself. It is that simple."

"Really Lord?" Fr. De Mello said.

"Sure Tony," Jesus replied and continued: "The more *completely* we become ourselves, the more pleased God is."

"I guess Lord, from looking with you *from* the Cross, we can also share in your ability to recognize the barriers that get in the way of people becoming fully themselves."

"That's so true Tony. I'm grateful to you for telling people in your books that every tenet, whether religious or secular, that counters anyone's journey to becoming fully who they are, needs to be vigorously opposed."

"You know, Lord, I appreciate your saying that. It's why I got to writing and giving retreats. I know from looking out from your Cross, that we are called to give our whole-hearted support to the attainment of each child's vocation to be fully human, independent, free and complete."

Jesus answered. "I'm so glad that you did write all that you did. You helped people attain their own special human fulfillment."

Both men stopped speaking.

Tony could see how intensely his Savior felt about helping each child of God reach completion. He felt strongly that Jesus passionately opposed each proposal that was willing to sacrifice on the altar of dogma, anyone's vocation to reach his or her personal human completion.

Fr. De Mello spoke softly but with immense feeling. "Looking out with you Jesus, from your

Cross, makes us want to encourage the advancement and drive of each person to complete the vocation to attain joy-filled humanity."

"Thank you, Tony," Jesus said. "And, I want to emphasize to you that there is only one heresy. It is this: to assert that any philosophy, political theory, religion or tradition takes precedence over human beings reaching their complete potential. My viewpoint from this hill overlooking Jerusalem and the world, affirms that all human persons have a sacred calling to become *fully themselves*."

"Thank you Lord: The gift of being oneself: You give us this. You became fully yourself. You became fully the person you are."

Jesus stood up and stretched the same legs that were nailed to the Cross, all those years ago, on that Friday afternoon. He asked a favor from Fr. De Mello. "Tony, tell me again that story about the boy at the Country Fair."

"OK Lord," Fr. De Mello answered.

"A little boy was watching a man selling balloons at a Country Fair. This man allowed a red balloon to break loose and soar up into the air. Next, he released a blue balloon, then a yellow one, and finally a white one. They all went soaring up into the sky until they disappeared.

"The little boy stood looking at a black balloon for a long time and then asked, 'Sir, if you sent this one up, would it go as high as the others?'

"The man gave the boy an understanding smile. He snapped the string that held the black balloon in place. As it soared upward, he said, 'It isn't the color, son. It's what's *inside* that makes it rise.'"

Jesus said: "I love that story. My father yearns for everyone's ability to soar and rise into the fullness of themselves and asked me to show people how to do this."

Fr. De Mello sat down. He said nothing for several minutes as he looked out from Calvary, with Jesus, over the human family. "Lord, I'd like to tell you what I believe is the meaning of your *incarnation*."

"Sure, Tony, tell us."

Fr. De Mello spoke softly with noted reverence:

"You became human. You became yourself."

Jesus nodded. "You're absolutely right Tony. I ended up on Calvary from being true to myself."

Fr. De Mello said: "And Lord, in your agony, you turned to the man dying next to you and promised to take him home that evening."

Jesus smiled and asked Fr. De Mello. "And what attracted me to him?"

Fr. De Mello was silent.

"Tony, it was simply the man *himself!* Remember what my friend Paul wrote to the Colossians (Col 2: 9–10):

> *The full content of divine nature lives in Christ, in his* humanity*, and you have been given full life in union with him.*

"I'm passionately and infinitely in love with each person. This is because I share human nature with them."

Jesus took a deep breath and continued. "Tony, I want each woman, each man, each child, to get this e-mail from me: 'There is nobody; there never has been anybody and there will never be anyone that I love more than I love you. There never will be anyone that I want in Heaven with me more than I want you, at my side, in my arms, in my heart forever. I love you. I don't love anyone more than I love you. I don't love my Father more than I love you.' And Tony, I want my message to get to everyone with the help of writers and preachers like yourself. You know, from all the time you have spent looking out with me from the Cross, that salvation comes to people who rejoice in the wholeness and completion of their humanity. That joy leads them to treasure their own sacredness and the sanctity of each other person."

Fr. De Mello thought about what Jesus said and, after a long pause, spoke. "Lord, I must admit that I often get upset responding to the news of the day. It is evident that in our society too many young people are missing out on their calling from God to become fully human, fully themselves. The Sunday newspaper recently showed a picture of youths who are members of gangs. From being in communion with you, Lord Jesus, I found myself wanting to assist those young people fulfill *their* vocations and grow into their true selves. You have taught me that God wants the process of becoming fully human to continue in them."

Jesus held Fr. De Mello's hands in his own. He looked straight at his Jesuit friend's eyes and spoke slowly and deliberately: "Tony, the world, the human race, doesn't need *Catholic* or *Protestant* or *Judaic* or *Islamic* theology or any theology except human theology."

Fr. De Mello asked, "Lord, is saying we need *human* theology, the same as saying we need your theology?"

"Yes, it is." Jesus answered. "I didn't become Catholic, Baptist or Buddhist. I became *human. I became myself.* I didn't become conservative, socialist or libertarian. I became *human*. I became *myself*. And that is all that my Father asks of anyone: *Become fully human, fully yourself.* But wait! I see two Franciscan friends approaching who understand the importance, for the process of becoming fully human, to nurture a deep *reverence for self.*"

5

Reverence for Self

Saint Francis of Assisi (September 26, 1181 – October 3, 1226) was the founder of the Order of Friars Minor, more commonly known as the Franciscans. He is known as the patron saint of animals, birds, and the environment, and it is customary for Catholic churches to hold ceremonies honoring animals around his feast-day of October 4.

RANCIS OF ASSISI came back on the Hill. Anthony of Padua followed Francis and spoke to people who were on a pilgrimage to Calvary.

"The only thing you have to do for Jesus is to be your own true self. Jesus came to save us. That means he came to bring us the confidence to be secure and at peace simply by being who we are. This means we have to be reverent towards ourselves. Just as there is no room in the heart of Jesus for thoughts of hate, we must not allow any hate to take root in our hearts, including hateful thoughts

SAINT ANTHONY OF PADUA was born around the year 1195 AD. Against the wishes of his family, Anthony entered a monastery near Lisbon, Portugal. He preached the Gospel throughout Lombardy, a region in northern Italy. He was a scholar and teacher; but it was as a preacher that Anthony was best known. He was canonized a saint on May 30, 1232, by Pope Gregory IX. He is often depicted holding the child Jesus.

about ourselves. This is crucial. Evil forces urge us to stagnate in self-destructive recollections. It seems they succeeded with Judas, who betrayed Jesus, but failed with Peter whom Jesus appointed head of the Apostles. I was going to say that they failed miserably with Peter, but it is more accurate to state that they failed *gloriously* with Peter. Jesus knew a thing or two, when he said, 'You are Peter and upon this rock, I will build my church.' (Matthew 16:18) Jesus found in Peter the person on whom to build his church, *because he found in Peter a man who turned to God for healing.* Peter did indeed express sorrow for his weakness but did not fall into depression. *Instead he relied on God."*

While Anthony was still speaking, Peter returned to Calvary. "Thank you Anthony. You're quite right! Jesus picked Paul and me knowing we wouldn't wallow in self-hatred out of shame for our weakness. Putting oneself down is really a form of pride arising from a refusal to accept the need for divine healing."

Paul joined them. "Yes, dear Pilgrims, Peter is correct. Jesus was able to knock *me* off my high horse of pride. I hope you remember, from an earlier conversation, how I was jolted on the road to Damascus and fell to the ground. I came down a peg or two, I can tell you; but the whole experience brought me to know Jesus' healing power of love and share his view of me from the Cross. Think about it. You can read in Luke's Acts of the Apostles how I assisted in the murder of Stephen, who was the first person to die for his faith in Jesus. I had people leave their jackets and overcoats in my care, while they stoned Stephen to death. One might have expected me to indulge in never-ending self-flagellation out of guilt and shame for my part in Stephen's murder. Instead, with the help of Stephen's prayers, I joined him in giving every fiber of my being to Jesus' gospel of all-conquering love. This gospel depends on reverence for self *and* the *freedom* to be oneself."

6

Freedom

Saint Thomas More: born 7 February, 1478: died 6 July, 1535. He was Lord Chancellor of England from 1529 to 1532. He refused to accept King Henry VIII's claim to be supreme head of the Church of England. This decision led to his execution for treason. He was canonized a saint in 1935. More was added to the Church of England's calendar of saints in 1980.

SAINT THOMAS MORE sat on a bench alongside Jesus on the hill of Calvary. He read out loud from a book by Thomas Hart: *The Art of Christian Listening* (p.66.)

> *The Christian economy is an economy of freedom. The point has sometimes been lost. If we go back to the prescriptions of Jesus for the life God wants us to live, what we find is simple and basic, with the particulars left up to ourselves. The Father of Jesus Christ is not a God of constraints but a God of freedom. He takes our maturity seriously, and, after a few simple directives, leaves our lives in our own hands.*

"I like that." Jesus said. "It reminds me how my parents were frantic with worry when they couldn't find me, while returning home from a visit to Jerusalem. When they found me in the Temple, they asked, 'Son, how could you put us through so much anxiety?' I told them, 'Didn't you know that I *had* to be about my Father's business?' I know it seems a bit cheeky the way dear Luke condensed his account of what happened. I do remember, however, even at that young age, being very conscious of what my Father hoped I would achieve on earth.

"My Father's business on this planet then and now is *providing the freedom necessary for human beings to grow*. The reality is that everyone is born to be free. Unfortunately, all sorts of institutions, philosophies, social theories, sects and religious groups have sought to *control* the lives of people. They forget that a human being *must be free* to develop."

Thomas More was overjoyed to be having this conversation with Christ about the meaning of life. His own thinking had matured greatly since the writing of his famous book *Utopia*. "We use the word 'salvation,' Lord, describing what you brought us. I see now, looking out from your Cross, that it simply means the process of bringing people to full human growth and *freedom*. I'm going to say something now, dear Jesus, that I would not have said when I was Chancellor of England."

Jesus responded: "OK Thomas, out with it. I'm very curious to know what it is you want to say. Is it about me?"

"Yes, Lord," Thomas replied: "It is this. You are a *humanist.* If you went for election, your slogan would be "Vote for me, Jesus. I'm for every woman. I'm for every man."

Jesus said: "Indeed Thomas, you are so right. Here from my risen view from the Cross, I look out with a longing for each child of my Father to be *free*."

"Yes, Lord," Thomas said with enthusiasm, "free to be ourselves. Thank you so much for bringing us that freedom."

He stopped speaking. He continued looking out from Calvary alongside his Savior. He thought to himself. "This is Jesus' viewpoint. Our Lord wants each child in Tijuana, Mexico and Omaha, Nebraska, to grow up fully. In order for that to happen they all need freedom. That's Jesus' viewpoint."

Thomas realized that Christ has the same vision for each Afghani and each Iraqi as he has for every English person, every American. He turned to Jesus and said: "Your hope, Lord, isn't it — that on our planet there will be universal freedom?"

Jesus said: "Yes, Thomas, but I leave to my followers, in every generation, the details for bringing my vision to reality. I remind them, from my view from the Cross, that they are responsible for nourishing the freedom of every person."

Jesus smiled. He could see how his words affected his English friend. "Thomas, a penny for your thoughts!"

"Well Lord," Thomas said, "I see that we human beings need to be aware that you want us to be totally free to express our faith in whatever we believe. You want no one to *impose* any sort of dogma on anyone else. I didn't fully appreciate that when I was the King's officer. I know now that everyone feels resentment when they are threatened by a *forced* imposition of another person's religious, political or philosophical stance. *Any restriction of human freedom is 100% contrary to your Father's Will.*"

Jesus said: "I'm very glad that you, Thomas, a man who appreciates the rule of law, affirms that it does not matter where attempts to limit human freedom come from. Of course there must be law governing any society, but *law must always respect human freedom*. I look forward to a conversation later this afternoon, here on Calvary, on the subject of law. But let me emphasize now that every rule, canon, by-law, interpretation, moral principle, dogma, regulation and tradition that attempts to *restrict human freedom is not compatible with the view from my Cross.*"

Thomas could see how intensely Christ felt about human freedom.

Jesus warmed up to his theme.

"There is a struggle going on in everyone from the first moment of that person's being. There are no exceptions. It is not possible for anyone to be without struggle, just as it is *not possible* for the river *not* to flow into the ocean. Let me share a story from my good friend Father Anthony de Mello.

"A boy was playing in his back garden. He

picked up a caterpillar. He had learned in school that the caterpillar, once it breaks out of the cocoon, becomes a butterfly. He was a kind and helpful boy, so he thought that his good deed for the day would be to help free the caterpillar to get on with its journey to becoming a butterfly. He gently broke the shell off the cocoon and released the caterpillar.

"That, Thomas, was the end of the caterpillar, and the end of any hope it had of becoming a butterfly. The very struggle to break free from the cocoon was the creator's evolutionary design for strengthening the developing wings on the caterpillar. When the time was right, the butterfly could fly away to a whole new life of freedom. It is being free to work through a process, that enables worthwhile growth to take place and lasting freedom to be achieved."

Jesus went on. "Thomas, the Big Bang of *redeemed* creation that happened on this Hill is an explosion into an infinite expansion of freedom. *Any* fiddling with that endowment of liberty is unacceptable to a person viewing reality from the Cross, the center of the redeemed universe."

Just as Jesus finished speaking, a new visitor, a man, came to Calvary. "*Guten Tag* everyone!"

Thomas More turned around to see who it was who had come to join them. It was the great German pastor, Dietrich Bonhoeffer.

Thomas got off the bench where he and Jesus were sitting together. He stood to greet this great German. He knew how Pastor Bonhoeffer had preached without compromise, from the early nineteen thirties, on the tragic consequences that would

DIETRICH BONHOEFFER (February 4, 1906 – April 9, 1945) was a German Lutheran pastor, theologian, participant in the German Resistance movement against Nazism, and a founding member of the Confessing Church. He was arrested in March 1943, imprisoned, and eventually hanged just before the end of World War II in Europe.

come from accepting the insane picture of life that Adolf Hitler used to destroy human freedom.

Jesus, still sitting down, looked up and said: "Everyone, this is Dietrich, my very dear German friend. He died because he closed his eyes long enough to *look out from here,* from my Cross on Calvary. My Father and I depend on all of those who, like him, invite people to share their clear vision of the universe of freedom and human development that I died to give everyone."

Dietrich stood there next to Jesus and Thomas and said: "Standing here, dear Lord and dear Chancellor Thomas, we can say with Dr. Martin Luther King, *'Free at last:'* Free: Imagine that! Free from fear, free from anxiety and *especially free from indifference,* but *not* free from pain."

"Yes, Dietrich," Jesus said in agreement, "the pain and the struggle will continue until my mission of bringing *complete human freedom to every child is accomplished.* For that to happen there must be in place the best possible *structure and government."*

7

Structure and Government

THOMAS AQUINAS (c. 1225 – 7 March 1274) was an Italian priest of the Dominican Order. He was a philosopher and theologian and his influence on Catholic thinking is still very profound. He is honored as one of the thirty-three Doctors of the Church.

JESUS HAD GONE off for a walk with his Father.

Some friends of his gathered on Calvary, waiting for Jesus to join them after his walk. One of them, the Apostle Matthew, spoke:

"Our mandate from Jesus is to promote the full realization of each person's potential."

ST. MATTHEW: He wrote a gospel and was one of Jesus' twelve apostles.

Another friend of Jesus responded with surprise. It was Thomas Aquinas.

"I didn't know Matthew that you were into the Greek idea of the fulfillment of potency."

"Certainly I am. I described how Jesus looks forward to welcoming us: 'When I was hungry, you gave me food. You shared *yourself* with me. When I was thirsty, you gave me something to drink. You shared *yourself* with me. When I was in prison, in hospital, in the nursing home, you cared for me."

Matthew looked up. Someone had tapped him on the shoulder. It was Jesus, back from his walk with his Father. "I want to thank you again, Matthew. You recorded my feelings very well. I wanted people to hear me tell them 'You shared *yourself* and you fused your humanity with mine. You fulfilled your vocation to be human. By becoming fully the unique person you are, you really helped *me*, in all the sisters and brothers for whom you cared.'"

Jesus paused as he saw another friend approach. "Hullo John"

It was John XXIII, who had gathered the bishops together for the Second Vatican Council.

He greeted Jesus and then turned to Matthew. "May I remind you, Matthew, that as Pope, I was greatly influenced by your gospel when I got the idea of having a Council. We needed to promote the structure of society that would best facilitate and enhance human growth. Church spires beckon us to foster the reach for the sky of children so that they come to their artistic, musical, mechanical and mental capability."

Blessed John XXIII was born Angelo Giuseppe Roncalli on November 25, 1881. He died on June 3, 1963. He was the 261st Pope of the Catholic Church and declared "Blessed" on September 3, 2000. His feast day is October 11 in the Catholic Church. He is also commemorated on June 3 by the Evangelical Lutheran Church in America and on June 4 by the Anglican Church of Canada.

Jesus was very happy to listen to his friends and didn't speak. The physician Luke, who wrote a gospel and history of the early church, spoke up: "I agree, Pope John. This is all clear from the Cross. From here, there is no blurred vision. This enables us to look for the *structure of human society* that will best ensure every child the opportunity to freely grow into the person that she or he is capable of becoming."

An American joined them. It was Father John Courtney Murray S. J.

He shared their enthusiasm for helping Jesus to construct God's Kingdom on earth. "God has in mind a structure to evolve for our human community. It is described in the Third book of Isaiah. (Isaiah 65: 17-21)"

Jesus spoke. "Father Murray, I'm impressed. Remind us what the ancient Hebrew prophet Isaiah says."

The American Jesuit read from his Bible.

Thus says the Lord:

Lo, I am about to create new heavens

And a new earth;

JOHN COURTNEY MURRAY (1904-1967): Jesuit priest: he helped persuade the Church to adopt the Second Vatican Council's Declaration on Religious Liberty.

The things of the past shall not be remembered
Or come to mind.
Instead, there shall always be rejoicing and
happiness
In what I create;
For I create Jerusalem to be a joy
And its people to be a delight;
I will rejoice in Jerusalem
And exult in my people.
No longer shall the sound of weeping be heard
there,
Or the sound of crying.
No longer shall there be in it
An infant who lives but a few days,
Or an old man who does not round out his full
lifetime;

He dies a mere youth, who reaches but a hundred years,
And he who fails of a hundred shall be thought accursed.
They shall live in the house they build,
And eat the fruit of the vineyards they plant.

Fr. Murray closed his Bible and said. "Lord may I expound on the text?"

Jesus smiled. "John, of course you may."

Fr. Murray continued. "Depending on philosophical and political leanings, different plans will be proposed for building the structure of society that is best for securing human welfare. That debate will continue. Looking out from Calvary with you, Lord, no matter what approach we take, we know that the structure of human society can be magnificent beyond description."

The others were impressed. They agreed with this scholarly American. Alongside Christ, aware of Isaiah's panorama, it was impossible for them not to be concerned about the flaws in community-building that produce inadequate environments for human development.

Jesus spoke. "I heartily endorse your concerns, as you look out with me from Calvary over the human family. You are aware, as I am, of my Father's invention of generosity and creation out of emptiness. During my public ministry, before coming here to Calvary, I spoke continuously about the impossibility of developing healthy human communities while entertaining greed. Luke and Matthew, you recalled how I pointed out a widow who gave the little she had to support the Temple in Jerusalem. She sacrificed all for the good of the community, even though her donation might be squandered by the greed of those in power.

"From the many hours you have shared my view from the Cross, you have learned that human life can only prosper when we share with one another and share with unbounded self-emptying generosity."

Fr. John Courtney Murray asked, "Lord, could I try to expound on what you are saying?"

Jesus smiled: "Of course John."

Fr. Murray stood up and spoke: "Governments need to fulfill their responsibility to promote the welfare of every citizen. Looking out from the Cross, there cannot be any argument that everyone deserves the best possible health care. Nor, while standing on Calvary, can there be any disputing that everyone should be able to have decent housing. It is likewise impossible, while sharing our Lord's view, to deny that government is responsible for ensuring that every citizen can procure adequate food, drink, clothing and whatever else is needed to provide for a dignified human existence. Government is only legitimate in proportion to its commitment to uphold the *value* of each and every citizen."

Fr. Murray sat down and the physician Luke stood up. He turned to Jesus and spoke. "Lord, you must know of a lady named Anita Roddick, who died in 2007. She was the founder and president of Body Shop, a cosmetics company. She wrote: 'I don't want our success to be measured only by financial yardsticks . . . What I want to be celebrated for . . . is how good we are to our employees and how we benefit our community . . . Look what the Quakers did . . . They looked after their employees — they provided houses, even built towns. They were honorable people; they didn't take more out of the business than they put in. They made profits of course. But they didn't tell lies, and they valued labor. That's an attitude we should get back to . . . People . . . are saying, 'I want to work for a company that values me, . . . I want to work for a company that enhances the human spirit, creates friendships, gives me a sense of being alive' . . ."

Jesus now stood up and looked at them intently for a full minute before speaking: "Every person's freedom to reach full human potential requires safety from the forces of greed and envy. The growth of *everyone's* standard of living demands protection from the chicanery and cheating that is designed to favor the few at the expense of the majority. In our search from Calvary for the best possible structure of human society we must recognize that the legal system must always promote the well-being and the freedom to grow, of *every* person and not just a select few."

Thomas Aquinas waited for Jesus to sit down and then stood up and spoke. "I've learned to look at our human family afresh each day from where our dear Savior died. From Calvary, we look at the environment and the structure of human society. We see huge shopping malls emerge and neighborhoods disappear. Human welfare decreases from the loss of belonging to a neighborhood community. The disintegration of towns, villages and cities puts in jeopardy the *human* growth of each person."

Aquinas turned to Jesus. "Lord, you went down to Nazareth to grow up at home. You had neighbors. People knew you. They recognized you when you came home and got up to speak in the local synagogue."

John Courtney Murray looked up from his seat. "You're right Thomas. I look from here at my own country. I can tell that people all over America experience nostalgia for the availability of shops and enterprises that were peculiar to their own home town. The rapacity of retail chains has blighted increasing areas of our land. This is so much the case that neighborhood retail business has suffered near extinction."

Thomas Aquinas looked at the American Jesuit and said: "Yes, John, I know what you are saying is true. We humans need communities of people who share their trades, crafts and unique talents as well as enjoying one another's company in our homes. The structure of each hamlet, village, town and city can be such as to enhance the likelihood of each girl and each boy reaching their full potential. I read that in northern Vermont, in your country, local authorities decided not to grant a permit for a large chain store to be built. The assessment was made after public hearings that more harm than good would result if the store were built. That's striking isn't it? A decision was made based on what was best for the structure of that community."

Jesus spoke after Aquinas sat down. "You all know now, from sharing my view, that the job of government is to maximize the potential of each person. Every government's mandate is to provide the best conditions for each little baby to reach her or his full humanity. My church's work is to foster restructuring society for the benefit of *all* people. I died to restructure society."

Jesus paused.

There was silence. Somehow they knew this was a time for them to wait for their Lord to speak again. He did. "I don't care who people put in—Green Party, Democrats, Republicans, whoever, as long as every child in the USA or in any other country is fully covered for whatever health care that child needs. I want the same for every adolescent, for every woman, for every man. Good government makes it possible for any youngster who is gifted to do so, to have the opportunity to learn to play a Mozart piano or violin sonata. Good government fosters whatever promotes the unity of the person and whatever builds up the cohesion of the community."

All his friends waited for Jesus to draw a breath. He continued. "When government is truly good, every child can grow up to enjoy, if she or he wishes it, a Beethoven trio, a garden lily of Monet, a gothic tower at York, the sound of a cat purring or a wave crashing. My Father and I, and our Spirit, want every generation to enjoy the best environment possible for humans to grow beautifully. The *measure* of how good or worthwhile any endeavor is: does this activity benefit human persons? In order to make that assessment, human beings need a profound respect for *Law*."

8

Law

JEROME, THE GREAT fourth-century scripture scholar, was lecturing to a group on Calvary.

"The Book of Deuteronomy (Greek *deuteros,* second) gives us a repetition, or second version of the laws given in the Book of Exodus. It reminds the king of the law's importance. 'He must write a copy of this Law on a scroll, at the dictation of the levitical priests. It must never leave him, and he must read it every day of his life and learn to fear Yahweh his God by keeping all the words of this Law and observing these rules . . . ' (Deuteronomy 17:18, 19, Jerusalem Bible)

"This instruction comes from a tradition that there should be a *copy* of the law, a *deuteros* or *second version* in everyone's *heart and soul.* In Matthew's gospel, 22: 35–40, we read:

JEROME (ca. 347 – September 30, 420) is best known as the translator of the Bible from Greek and Hebrew into Latin.

> *One of them, a scholar of the law, tested him by asking, 'Teacher, which commandment in the law is the greatest?' He said to him, 'You shall love the Lord, your God, with all your heart, with all your soul, and with all your mind. This is the greatest and the first commandment. The second is like it. You shall love your neighbor as yourself. The whole law and the prophets depend on these two commandments.*

"Jesus, through his love of God and his love of others as himself, absorbed into *his heart and soul* a second or *deuteros* copy of the *whole law*. Looking out from the Cross keeps a true *deuteros* version of the law of love in ourselves."

Jerome continued. "Jesus, looking out from Calvary, envisions a rule of law that ensures for every child and grown-up adequate health-care, housing, nourishment, clothing, education, recreation, artistic development and beauty of environment. Jesus knows that we need the rule of law to show reverence for ourselves and for others. The

PIERRE TEILHARD DE CHARDIN (May 1, 1881 – April 10, 1955) was a French Jesuit priest. He was a scientist who studied the origins of the human race.

rule of law is seen to be a system of protection for the freedom and well-being of each citizen."

One of those listening to Jerome was Teilhard de Chardin, the French Jesuit anthropologist.

He spoke. "Jerome, I like what you are saying about the rule of law. I was buried in upstate New York. New York State has a law that says that a car's headlights must be switched on whenever the weather demands the use of windshield wipers. Although it is commonly ignored, it is a good law. In Canada, the law demands that headlights be on for *all* driving. This enhances the safety of other drivers. When headlights are used, people are much more aware of other cars on the road. The number of automobile accidents is

ST. JOHN FISHER (C. 1469 – 535), was bishop of Rochester in England. He was executed for not accepting King Henry VIII as head of the Church of England.

reduced. The rule of law has been used to encourage good choices for everyone's welfare."

St. John Fisher, Bishop of Rochester in England got up to speak. "We humans cannot survive in chaos. In Robert Bolt's play, *A Man For All Seasons*, my good friend, Thomas More, Chancellor of the Kingdom, tells his future son-in-law that England is planted with a system of laws. One needs to be careful about uprooting any of them for fear of the anarchy that could ensue. When a community has experienced anarchy and chaos, people are appreciative of the return to the rule of law."

Jerome nodded in agreement and said. "Yes, John. Such was the case in Israel as described in the Bible, in the Book of Nehemiah: 8:3.

Standing at one end of the open place that was before the Water Gate, he (Ezra) read out of the

GILBERT KEITH CHESTERTON (May 29, 1874 – June 14, 1936) was an English Catholic whose writings continue to exercise a strong influence in the Church.

book from daybreak till midday, in the presence of the men, the women, and those children old enough to understand: and all the people listened attentively to the book of the law.'"

The Englishman, G. K. Chesterton, was in the group. He spoke. "If you don't mind, I'll stay sitting. May I draw your attention to Charles Dickens' *Oliver Twist.* I'm sure you have all read it by now. You remember how Oliver's benefactor, Mr. Brownlow, tells Bumble that as far as the law is concerned, a wife acts in obedience to her husband.

"Bumble, who has always been bossed about by his wife, remarks, 'If the law supposes that, the law is an ass.'"

Chesterton continued. "Unfortunately, the law can indeed become idiotic when it loses sight of what can be seen from the Cross: that *the humanity of each citizen comes first* when considering legislation."

An American, John Foster Dulles rose and addressed the group. He had been Secretary of State during the presidency of Dwight D. Eisenhower from 1953 to 1959 and the father of a well-know American Jesuit, Cardinal Avery Dulles. "I would like to share some history from my country as long as we are discussing the subject of Law. "Judge John Marshall Harlan (1833–1911) was appointed by President Rutherford B. Hayes (1822-93) to the United States Supreme Court and served for thirty-four years. Upholding the Thirteenth and Fourteenth Amendments in a minority of one dissenting opinion he denounced the Court's acceptance of 'separate but equal' schools.

"He wrote: 'In the view of the Constitution, in the eye of the law, there is in this country no superior, dominant, ruling class of citizens. There is no caste here. Our Constitution is color-blind, and neither knows nor tolerates classes among citizens.

In respect of civil rights, all citizens are equal before the law. The humblest is the peer of the most powerful."

(Dissenting opinion, Plessy v. Ferguson 163 U.S. 537, 559 [1896])

Everyone fell silent as Jesus, himself, now rose to speak. "Thank you John. I am *eternally grateful* to Judge Harlan for his courage in vigorously opposing the exclusion of anyone from the protection of law. Law comes into our lives in different forms. For our survival we need the law of gravity and every other law of our physical universe. We also need the *law of the survival of the fittest.* For me and my Father, the 'fittest' are *all* the children and *all* the grown-ups *without exception. All* of them: I, Christ, have survived all the pain experienced in our universe by every child, every woman and every man. I have ushered in the new eternal era championing the survival of the fittest, which means I have lived and died for *everybody*. Looking out from the Cross, you join me in expecting that those in Government will fulfill their responsibility to provide for the survival of the fittest, the survival of *every person.* They will do this by keeping safe in their minds, in their hearts and in their souls a *deuteros,* a second and entire copy of the Law. They must remember what I told all of you over and over. The entire Law is summed up in the command. 'Love one another as you love yourselves and love your Creator.' This universal law of love is founded on the *Unity of the Human Family.*"

9

Unity of the Human Family

IT WAS A day when people who had lived their lives in the twentieth century were together looking out from Calvary over the human family. One of those present was the Australian Frank Sheed. He and his wife Maisie Ward had spent their lives sharing Jesus' view from the Cross through their book-publishing company Sheed & Ward.

Frank was speaking. "In contrast to Jesus' outlook from Calvary of universal love, our poor world is continually faced with danger from the *selective pretense* of love. Jesus' love *is not* selective. Risen from his pain, he has a clear view of every time, every space, *every person*. He *takes in* everyone. He saw the picture of the child in the mid-East, on the

FRANK SHEED (1897-1981) and MAISIE WARD (1897-1981): They were a married couple and both were prominent religious writers: In 1926 they founded the Catholic publishing house of Sheed & Ward.

front of a news magazine, carrying a make-believe weapon of violence. He looked into each gas chamber in Auschwitz where his Father's children, his own kindred, were being gassed. He could clearly see, on August 15, 1998, during sectarian violence in Ireland, each of the bombers in the town of Omagh, and each of their victims. He can see whose lands were stolen in Palestine. He can see each opposing group of our human family. This enmity between people grieves the heart of Jesus. Every war and conflict hinders the Father's creative evolution of love that was targeted to bring every person to personal fulfillment in the *unity of the human family.*"

Frank's wife Maisie spoke next. "It was common not that long ago for hospitals to ask patients who were being admitted, to fill out a form that included spaces indicating date of birth, sex, and race. At least one patient wrote in 'human.' In the creation accounts of the Book of Genesis it is clear that just *one* human race came *into being.* Because the *unity of the human* race has been lost sight of, savage conflicts continue between people from different cultures even though they share *being human* in common.

Jesus had joined them. "Yes, Maisie, one sees this clearly from the Cross. Every effort is magnificent that helps establish an environment holding sacred the eternal and priceless beauty of each person. It is also transparent to anyone alongside me on Calvary, that every thought, word or deed

POPE JOHN PAUL II was born Karol Jozef Wojtyla on 18 May, 1920. He died 2 April, 2005. He was the 264th Pope of the Catholic church.

that holds cheap the humanity of *anybody*, is to be rejected."

John Paul II waited for Jesus to sit down and then rose to speak.

"Lord Jesus, your victory has set in stone, in plant, in brain, in art, in music, in every time, place, situation, in every family, country and ocean the eternal loveliness of moving away from the destruction of any human being. It is your view Lord, from Calvary, and ours beside you, that every human person is precious and worth living and dying for."

Ignatius of Loyola rose to speak.

"Yes, John Paul, our obligation to love God flows from our recognizing how beautiful we have been knit by God in our mother's womb. From appreciating with gratitude that life-giving love, we appreciate both ourselves and our beloved neighbor. There is *not one* human being more valuable than another. There is *not one* human being less valuable than another. This *unity of the human family* is real. It is borne out by science. We are one *human race* and *one* only. *This* is *reality*."

SAINT IGNATIUS OF LOYOLA (1491 – 1556), was the principal founder and first Superior General of the Society of Jesus, a religious order of the Catholic Church professing direct service to the Pope. Members of the order are called Jesuits.

10

Reality

ST. CATHERINE OF SIENA. Detail of a work by Domenico Beccafumi, c. 1515.

Saint Catherine of Siena (March 25, 1347 – April 29, 1380) was a lay member of the Dominican Order. She exercised great influence for the good of the Church during her lifetime.

ATHERINE OF SIENA spoke to a group of recently deceased people who had gathered with her to share the view from Jesus' Cross.

"Jesus didn't get ahead of himself. He didn't attempt resurrection ahead of his facing reality. He faced pain. He knew he had to go to Jerusalem and suffer, in order to show us reality clearly from the Cross. Before he could show us the view from Calvary, he needed to close down those other screens that had been set up to view a world that is not real. He continues to need our help in removing the graphics and images that show a false view of the world."

Monsignor Jack Egan from Chicago had come to the Hill with Catherine.

MONSIGNOR JACK EGAN (1916-2001): He worked all his life to improve life for all working people.

He had spent all of his life advocating for a proper environment for people to grow with good health care and a dignified standard of living. Catherine invited him to speak.

“Thank you Catherine. I found out that when the human family is viewed from some arbitrary vantage point as far away from the Cross as possible, a world economy is accepted that has come to depend on exploiting the labor of the weakest. The viewer alongside Jesus can never condone the trading in goods that are manufactured by people in inhuman conditions. There has to be a constant regression into *unreality,* for the profiteering to continue unchecked without any concern for the child, woman or man whose labor was abused. We see with Jesus from the Cross the madness of believing that we can prosper while turning our backs on reality. The *reality* is that each human person is precious and of more value than any social survey could measure.”

Monsignor Egan paused.

Catherine invited him to continue. “Go on, Jack.”

"All right then, Catherine, I will. When we view reality from the Cross, we are impelled to take up the quest for the sacred grail and ask: Why do we exist? From the Cross, the center of this and all other universes, the answer comes to us in unambiguous clarity. The *secret of our being* is that *we are loved*. We need to think through this carefully. We have evolved from a creative process that was initiated before *and* beyond space and time. There *had* to be, *has* to be and *will always have* to be *Being* for us to be, for us to *exist*. The view from the Cross opens our eyes to what *Being* is. We see that *Being* is *love*. That means simply that Being *wants* the *well-being* of all that is. In the Book of Chronicles we are told that we are 'irrevocably loved.' We are human beings. All of us: one human race of beings endowed with existence from Being. Being is God. God is Being. God is love and, out of the goodness of God's being came the original outpouring of creation, the invention of God's emptying and generosity of love."

The great Polish scientist Nicolaus Copernicus happened to be strolling nearby and heard Monsignor Egan talking.

NICOLAUS COPERNICUS (February 19, 1473 – May 24, 1543.) He was an astronomer who demonstrated that the Earth was not the center of the universe

He came over and Catherine invited him to speak. "Thank you, Catherine. From observations of supernova and other data, astronomers have been surprised by the speed of the universe's expansion. It doesn't come as a surprise when one looks out from Calvary. Our universe is expanding because of the blessedness of human lives seeing reality from the Real Presence of the Cross. Any one human being has immense power for good: It is possible for any person living in the present moment, to have an enriching effect on the universe that will be part of the expansion of reality into an unending future."

As Copernicus finished speaking, a familiar figure appeared and Catherine invited him also to speak. It was the great Ludwig Van Beethoven. He said to the group: "Listen to a Cole Porter song or an oratorio by Handel. They widen our universe. All the great artists do the same, not just we musicians. Jackson Pollock's paintings were unknown at one time. He extended our experience of reality."

There was a stir of excitement in the group when the 34th President of the United States, Dwight D. Eisenhower, came by.

"Good Morning, Mr. President," Catherine greeted him. "Please share some words of wisdom with us."

"Thank you dear," the great leader said. He went on: "There was a time when arbitrary rules imposed restrictions on the use of public transport. Then, during my presidency, Rosa Parks came along. She *knew* that it was wrong for her to be prevented from sitting in any available seat in a bus. It was evil

DWIGHT D. EISENHOWER (1890 – 1969): 34th President of the United States from 1953 until 1961.

because it denied the *reality* of her dignity as a person. Her courage enlarged all our hearts. My hope for America, and indeed for all the world, is that more and more people can share Rosa Parks' view from this Hill. Looking out from here it is inevitable that people will join with Rosa and cause our universe to expand in love with greater and greater speed."

The next person to arrive and join Catherine and her friends was the great bishop of Geneva, Francis de Sales.

Everyone listened to what this gentle man had to say. "If it came to pass, that governments had an appreciation of the view from the Real Presence on this Hill, there would be an extraordinary change in human society. The change would come from getting in touch with reality. Somehow it all means that the connection with the Real Presence has been broken. Even though the Presence is *real*, it can be ignored, denied, forgotten. When that happens, whoever is vulnerable suffers. And those who are vulnerable number in the countless millions. People

SAINT FRANCIS DE SALES (1567 – 1622) was bishop of Geneva, Switzerland. He was an accomplished preacher. He is known for his writings on the topic of spiritual direction and spiritual formation, including his Introduction to the Devout Life.

suffer from malnutrition, from hate, from wrongful imprisonment, from unemployment, from lack of proper medical care. So much of the suffering that people are experiencing comes from efforts to slow down or even stop the extension of love flowing out from this Hill. Why are children sold into prostitution? How can such an evil persist? How is it possible for a Scandinavian community to harbor a pedophile ring that takes advantage of the poverty in Eastern Europe? To keep our minds in touch with reality, it is helpful to *close* our eyes and *look out from the Cross.*"

Paul of Tarsus spoke, "Thank you Bishop Francis, I know what you are talking about. I had my eyes closed for me, when I fell to the ground. My mind was opened and I got a *clear picture* of reality. It wasn't always so. I used to be such a zealous Pharisee that I had substituted dogmatic certainty for reality. I had completely lost sight of divine compassion and gentleness. It was when I lost the use of my *physical* sight that I began to see reality clearly. I wrote to the people in Galatia,

> *United with you in the Lord, I am confident*
> *that you will not take the wrong view.*
> (Galatians 5:10)

"I spent the rest of my life encouraging people to *stay in the real world alongside Christ.*"

Peter came along and of course Catherine asked him to speak to the gathering.

"I, like Paul, needed to be jolted into *seeing reality alongside Jesus.* At the Last Supper, I said to Jesus, 'You will never wash my feet.' (John 13:8) Notice my negative *never.* I imagined that my darkroom undeveloped images, were accurate depictions of reality. I was *photographing* life and seeing the *negatives* as pictures of reality. My album of negatives made me think; 'I'm not good enough for Jesus to get involved in my life.' Jesus quickly brought me back to reality. 'If I do not wash you, you will have no share in my heritage.' I replied, 'Lord, then not only my feet, but my hands and head as well.' I had come to the clear view of reality we can all get, from remaining present here alongside Jesus sharing his view from the Cross. Beside him, I see the component of reality that Jesus reveals with unmistakable clarity — *emptying*; yes God's *invention of emptying.*"

11

The Invention of Emptying

IT WAS ANOTHER pleasant morning on Calvary. Jesus was taking another walk with his Father. A group of his friends were chatting together. One of them was Francis of Assisi. He was speaking to Anthony of Padua. "Anthony, can I tell you one really important thing I have learned from looking out across history from our Lord's cross?"

Anthony replied. "Now come on, Francis, you know I always want to know what's on your mind!"

"Well it's this, Anthony. I have learned that *God invented emptying.*

"Continue, Francis. I feel you're on to something crucially important."

"Yes, God's invention of emptying made our existence and the being of everything possible. Our universe is evolved out of the mystery of God's generosity. It has come into being from the emptying of God. Our universe and the other universes that we are yet to experience, come from the divine outpouring of utter unselfishness. Every generation is invited by God to *invent continually* better ways to promote the growth into freedom and fullness of each person."

Another friend joined them. It was Galileo Galilei.

"Francis, I couldn't help hearing what you were saying to Anthony about God inventing emptying. Inventive ingenuity helps all of us. We continue to benefit from the invention of the wheel. I was amused to learn that the French philosopher and mathematician, Blaise Pascal, invented the wheel-barrow. Did you know that his contemporary, another French philosopher, Rene Descartes, invented roulette? Around the same time, across the Channel in England, Sir John Suckling invented the game of cribbage."

John the Baptist, who introduced Jesus to the

GALILEO GALILEI (1564-1642): Italian mathematician, and astronomer: he was persecuted by Church authorities who resisted his scientific discoveries.

Jewish people, came to join them. He said. "I, too, if you don't mind my saying so, was inventive! I discovered a cure for anxiety. People came to me sharing their worries. I knew this from the question that many of them asked me. 'What *ought* we to do?' That word *ought* revealed anxiety. I discovered the antidote to worry. Share. I told soldiers and others to 'share and treat others, as you would like to be treated yourself.' I encouraged people to get rid of their anxiety by using *God's original invention of emptying and sharing."*

Anthony of Padua spoke. "Paul described in *Phillipians* 2: 5-9, how this divine invention of self-emptying is seen perfectly in Jesus.

> *Christ Jesus,*
> *Who, though he was in the form of God, did not regard equality with God something to be grasped.*
> *Rather, he emptied himself coming in human likeness; and found human in appearance, he humbled himself, becoming obedient to death,*

even death on a cross.
Because of this, God greatly exalted him.'"

Anthony went on. "Think about it. Jesus has risen. He did not hold on to anything. So, there was nothing to prevent his outpouring and self-emptying to carry his humanity beyond the grave. He wants to share with us the experience of resurrection into eternal freedom from possessiveness. He knows that from self-emptying we will be able to enjoy whatever our hearts desire."

It was at that moment that Oliver Plunkett from Ireland joined them.

Oliver had suffered like so many of Jesus' friends because of their commitment to God's invention of emptying and sharing generously.

ST. OLIVER PLUNKETT (1629-1681): Archbishop of Armagh, Ireland: died a martyr: declared a saint in 1975.

"Hello everyone; I heard your conversation while I was standing over there and I would like to share a story that can help us appreciate God's invention of self-emptying and holding onto nothing.

"The island of Innisfree inspired W. B. Yeats' famous poem:

> *I will arise and go now, and go to Innisfree*
> *I hear lake water lapping with low sounds by the shore.*

"An old man who lived on the island, came to the end of his life. Innisfree, for him, was a reflection of Heaven itself. Just as he was about to die, he reached down and clasped a handful of the earth of his beloved island. Saint Peter met him at the Gate of Heaven and said: 'Come in friend . . . but first you must let go of that handful of soil.'

'Never' said the old man.

"A long time went by.

"Peter came out again, this time bringing with him Ireland's own Saint Patrick.

"The old man was overjoyed to meet the great saint. Patrick said to him: 'Come in with me. We have some wonderful surprises in store for you, but first get rid of that soil that you are holding.'

"The old man again refused to let it go and stayed outside.

"Another long time passed. Then the Lord Jesus himself came out with Peter. 'Come in son,' He said, 'we all miss you. We have prepared something special for you.' By now the old man was feeble. Peter and the Lord helped him to his feet. In his weakness he lost his grip of the soil and it filtered out between his fingers.

"His hand was *empty*. He then entered Heaven and there before his eyes was his beloved Innisfree. The man had finally come to benefit from God's original invention of letting go."

"Good story, Oliver." It was the Lord Jesus back from his walk. "I wanted so much to tell everyone that emptying and letting go are components of the freedom that is at the core of divine nature and human nature. My Father asked me to come on

Earth to bring people into this divine freedom of emptying and letting go."

The friends of Jesus were silent. They all knew how he *emptied* himself totally. He *completely* rid himself of any possibility of possessiveness.

Francis of Assisi broke the silence. "Lord, we are able to see and touch in you the *emptying essence* of God that brought our universe and us into being."

Jesus stood up. "I'm going over to spend time with my mother and earthly father Joseph. Please go on with your conversation. This subject of my Father's invention of emptying is very important indeed."

They all stood up as Jesus left.

Luke the physician had been listening to their conversation from a little distance away. "I was listening to all of you talking about emptying and sharing. I started to imagine looking at an X-ray of Jesus' heart. It's what we *wouldn't* see there that's impressive. There would be no clutter, no hardening of the arteries of generosity from clinging onto stuff. If we looked deeply, *we wouldn't be able to find even one refusal* to reach out in love; not in Jesus' heart."

"You are so right Luke," Anthony of Padua agreed, "and that's what he's hoping will happen in our hearts. He staked his life on it. He believes that if he can share with us God's original invention of letting go and emptying, we can be free from the excess baggage of resentments, revenge and greed. Just as he was about to breathe his last breath, Jesus said, 'It is finished.' He's telling us. "I really completed the work, the job, into which I was incarnated. I have fully shared with you, *my Father's invention of emptying* so you can be free to be yourself.' "

A lady joined them. She was St Frances Xavier Cabrini, known as Mother Cabrini, who had spent her life in America.

"I heard you men talking while I was tending to the flowers. Thank you for reminding me that looking out from Calvary with Jesus enables us to see the blessing of God's original invention of emptiness and generosity that brought us all into being. Possessiveness can badly damage human freedom.

SAINT FRANCES XAVIER CABRINI (1850-1917): She was known as Mother Cabrini: She came to America and devoted her life to the care of the young.

In my adopted country, The United States of America, a treasured symbol of freedom is the Liberty Bell in Philadelphia, Pennsylvania. It has been damaged more than once. It was cracked at its first ringing after it was brought to America in 1752. It was recast but cracked again on July 8, 1835, while being tolled in memory of Chief Justice Marshall. Our own internal liberty and freedom is safe from been cracked or damaged when we use God's original invention of being empty of any possessiveness and greed. I think it is also important to remember that the component of evil that is most damaging to the full and free growth of each person is greed. We are able to look out from the Cross, with Jesus, knowing that our liberty and freedom are guaranteed by being unshackled from possessiveness and being *empty* of greed. Jesus reveals the attitude of mind that keeps us appreciative of God's *invention of emptying* from which reality emerged: *poverty*."

Francis of Assisi was back on Calvary. He spoke. "When greed gets preferential treatment, human completion suffers and evil results. Poverty as an attitude means what? Surely it means being *grateful* and seeing the absolute importance of *sharing*. It is great when anybody has an inner desire to *share whatever they have,* for improving the condition of every child."

Galileo spoke. “Scientists continue to probe back in time in the effort to better understand how our universe began. They speak of the Big Bang that happened way back when. Jesus shows us from Calvary that God’s great invention of being emptied of possessiveness exploded into bringing us and everything else into being. It is evident that *emptying* leads to a quality that Jesus tells us is a sure measurement of becoming fully human: *generosity*.”

12

Generosity

CARDINAL JOSEPH BERNARDIN spoke.

"What does it mean to be mature—to be grown-up? It must indicate development. I wonder if there is some method that we can rely on to accurately tell the degree of desirable growth in each human being?"

"Yes. There is," Jesus answered. Jesus went on to explain to the American churchman: "New embryonic states are experienced by each person, at many levels, with new emergence and fresh hatchings as days, months and years go by. I have found that there is a precise measurement to give the current readings of human development in each person. It is a universal gauge. It measures accurately a person's growth in kindness, considera-

JOSEPH LOUIS CARDINAL BERNARDIN (April 2, 1928 – November 14, 1996) was Archbishop of Chicago from 1982 until his death.

tion and thoughtful care of others' needs. I refer to the quality called generosity. Generosity: It takes practice to learn how to use this instrument for determining the stage reached by any individual in realizing her or his potential to fully grow up as a human person. Someone is approaching who, I'm sure, will help me explain."

Jesus had noticed another churchman approaching. This was Monsignor Ronald Knox.

From spending all that time translating the Bible, Knox was familiar with everything that was recorded about Jesus' life. "Yes, Lord, I caught what you were saying, as I came nearer. You are, indeed, very good at measuring how a person is maturing in

RONALD ARBUTHNOTT KNOX: (1888 - 1957) He was a Catholic priest. He single-handedly translated the St. Jerome Latin Vulgate Bible into English. He wrote books on religious themes and also detective fiction.

generosity. You can, with really amazing exactness, pinpoint the graph and curve of generosity in everybody. You said, for example, about your disciple, Nathaniel, also known as Bartholomew, 'There is no duplicity in him!' (John1:47) That meant, didn't it Lord, that you *knew* that Nathaniel was generous?"

"Yes, Ronald, you are quite right. Nathaniel, indeed, was without guile of any sort. There was no element of deception in him. He had overcome any trace of inner self-conflict. He was able, as a result, to rise to an astonishingly high altitude of kindness, consideration and thoughtfulness — in a word — generosity."

Cardinal Bernardin spoke: "I think, Lord, that examples would be helpful. I mean can you show us others who have shared Nathaniel's straightforward and one hundred per cent honest nature and reached high levels of generosity?"

Jesus showed his familiar smile: "Of course I can, Bernard. How about starting with yourself?"

"Oh, Lord, I didn't . . . " Cardinal Bernardin began, but Jesus interrupted him: "No, don't be embarrassed. I know of your generosity in fulfilling your ministry in Chicago and beyond. I remember your generosity in reconciling with someone who made false accusations against you. And look at Ronald's life too."

Now it was Monsignor Knox who turned red in the face: "Oh, Jesus, please."

"No, Ronald, false modesty is not helpful. OK, acknowledge the help of our Holy Spirit. But the fact is that you showed *extraordinary generosity* in sacrificing your own comfort and ease to complete your monumental undertaking of translating the whole Bible into English. It meant that you *had* to have reached, like your mentor, St. Jerome, a beautiful state of generosity in order to keep your mind focused on your work, as you poured over the original Greek, Hebrew and Aramaic texts as well as Jerome's Latin."

Cardinal Bernardin waited until Jesus had finished speaking. Then he said: "Our speaking about *generosity* reminds me, Lord, of your crying out on Good Friday, 'Father, forgive them for they do not know what they do.' In the generosity of your heart you could see how *alone and fragile* any of us can be."

13

Alone and Fragile

ENRI NOUWEN RETURNED to Calvary. He wanted to meet with a new group of pilgrims from Boston. He had known a lot of them at Harvard. They were happy to listen to him again. "Whenever a person makes a judgment, there is some error. There is some lack. More can be learned about the subject under scrutiny. Human judgment is *fallible*. It is most likely to approach accuracy when its fallibility is recognized and divine guidance is sought. This becomes supremely important when the subject under judgment is a human person. Jesus' judgment of another person is infallible. He knows that the vessel in which we carry impartial

HENRI NOUWEN (1932 – 1996) was a Dutch Catholic priest and writer who wrote 40 books on the spiritual life. *The Wounded Healer, In the Name of Jesus, Clowning in Rome, The Life of the Beloved* and *The Way of the Heart* are just a few of the more widely recognized titles.

judgment of another is delicate and tender; this precious vase in our souls protecting fairness and objectivity is constantly threatened by prejudice and narrow-mindedness.

"Jesus *knows and never forgets the loneliness* of each person. There is a universe of aloneness in each one of us. Instead of rushing to judgment like we all do too often, Jesus gently makes himself available to offer solace and healing to the lonely person. And that means *everybody!* There is loneliness in everyone. He knows how *alone and fragile* is the deepest inner self of each person. He knows our loneliness and our *pain.*"

14

Pain

PETER LOOKED OUT from Calvary. With Peter were Mary, Jesus' mother, her husband Joseph and Jesus himself. Peter remembered a report in the newspaper about the Milky Way crashing into another galaxy ten billion years ago. Peter said to them: "We look deep into the stars. *From the Cross* our search continues. At the core of the universe we are probing is the *pain of God.*"

Jesus said: "Yes, Peter; pain is still present—but it will end. It will end because the *reality* you see from the Cross, guarantees it to end. This *will* happen because God's Real Presence *and pain* on this hill initiated the constantly increasing speed of our universe to reach the resurrection of complete love."

Mary nodded in agreement: "Yes Peter; you need to get people to understand how immeasurable was my son's pain from what he saw—and continues to see from here."

Mary's husband Joseph, Jesus' foster father on Earth, now spoke: "Even though I died before my child, I shared his view from Heaven. It is the same view we see from the Cross. It takes in all of the pain that people continue to suffer from regimes that survive only by trampling on the human birthright of liberty. He saw the trains in the nineteen forties that carried men, women and children to the killing camps in Europe."

Peter turned to Jesus: "Lord, here on that Friday, you were held back by nails. You couldn't move. You could not stroke your forehead. You could not bend down to touch your legs. You couldn't move from where you were."

"Yes, Peter; that was how I died: unable to move from where I was. And yet, looking out from my Cross, I embarked on a world sightseeing tour that took in everyone, everyone that ever lived or will live, beginning with the man dying next to me. God's glory is never separated from my pain or from anyone's pain. There never will be a day when God does not wish to experience your and my wounds and to share in our journey of healing. My helplessness and terrible pain, including my deep feeling of abandonment, reveal God's power to you. God's *only* power is to love. That's all God can do; love. Close your eyes and look out from my Cross. We'll share our pains together—and *share our risen victory* together. I'll move in with you. I'm knocking. Open the door. I want you to welcome me into your *House and Home*."

15 House and Home

HOMAS MERTON CAME once again to join his friend Henri Nouwen. Henri invited Thomas to speak to the Boston pilgrims.

Thomas began, "The most sacred places on Earth are the inner depths of each person. Jesus recognized that inner sacredness in human beings. He thinks of each of us as his Father's house and home. When he was a boy of twelve, he said to his parents 'Did you not know that I had to be in my Father's house?' As he repeats these words to us today, he is speaking about his longing to be at home in each of us.

"St. Peter's in Rome, the sacred shrines of Mecca, the Jerusalem Wailing Wall — all the gravitational centers that attract the faithful of every tradition, pale into insignificance when placed next to the holiness of each human being. Jesus knew that. This knowledge kept him moving through all the pain that he experienced in his own humanity until he came to resurrection and established forever, beyond any possibility of eradication, the sacredness of every child, every man and every woman.

"Jesus' longing to be welcomed as a guest in each of us, was nurtured as he recited the psalms day after day.

> *O Lord I love the house where you dwell,*
> *The place where your glory abides.*
> (Psalm 26: 8)
> *I lift up my hands in prayer to your holy place.*
> (Psalm 28: 2b)
> *All you . . . who stand in the house of the Lord,*
> *. . . Lift up your hands to the holy place.*
> Psalm 134: 1b,2a)

"That's where Jesus knocks—on the door of that holy place, on the sinews of each of our minds, hearts and spirits. "Throughout the sixth week of each year, the Church uses this prayer: "To those who love you, Lord, you promise to come with your Son and make your home within them."

The Boston pilgrims were thrilled and delighted. Henri invited John to speak.

JOHN THE APOSTLE

John responded, "The first time some of us disciples met Jesus we asked him, 'Where are you staying?' (John 1: 38) In the Greek text, the word '*menein*' is used. It means more than just 'where is your house?' or 'where is your apartment?' or 'where is your present lodging?' The Greek means something like: 'Where are you *rooted?* What is the source of your being and meaning?' Or, as we might sometimes say; 'where are you *coming from?*' — what environment, what situation makes you comfortable and at ease?' It was a life-turning experience for us disciples, when Jesus revealed where he was most at home. He told us then what he tells everyone who comes to share his view from Calvary. He tells us that he wants to stay and settle down for good, *within each of us. There* is his *house and home.*"

Jerome the expert scripture scholar came to talk to the pilgrims. "Moses, who led the Jewish people out of Egypt, gives instructions in the Book of Deuteronomy for eating the Passover in the place designated by the Lord: in each person's *home.* All of us can experience daily, a constant Passover in our own homes, in our hearts and souls. There, within ourselves, we can celebrate the Passover from Egypt, leaving behind fear and anxiety knowing that our homes, *our selves* are secure and safe as we stand on the hill with Jesus."

"Thank you Jerome." It was Jesus. He too wanted to speak to the pilgrims from America. "The Cross of Calvary reveals to you the tragedy when the divine place that is each person, is violated. I took on responsibility for repairing the destruction that is done to anyone. I took upon myself the healing of each person's desecration. My Father asked me to perfectly reflect, express and mirror God's sadness for the violation of his temple, which is what every person is."

Jesus' mother had come with him to meet the pilgrims. She spoke. "When you get a hold of this, it changes everything. When you come to realize, looking out with Jesus from his vantage point on Calvary, that each of you is the house and home where God can feel comfortable, then your reverence for yourselves and for those around you increases infinitely. From that realization, comes your awareness of how sacred not only is your own locus but also, how in need of reverence is the location we call sister or brother. Jesus saw these sacred places from Gethsemane and from Calvary. He prayed for them and continues to pray for them. Jesus prays for you and for me — all the time. This kept him going: this love for these special homes and houses that are you and I. His constant *prayer* for each of us kept him going into Easter morning. He invites us to share in his *prayer*."

16 Prayer

EDITH STEIN (1891 – 1942) was a German Jewish philosopher who became a Catholic. She entered the Carmelite Order. Her warnings about Adolf Hitler and Nazism were ignored by the Pope and Church in the 1930s. She was taken from her convent in Holland and transported to a concentration camp where she was gassed to death. She was canonized as Saint Teresa Benedicta of the Cross (her Carmelite monastic name) by Pope John Paul II in 1998.

EDITH STEIN, WHO died in a concentration camp, addressed the friends of Jesus on Calvary.

"Our best praying begins with accepting Jesus' message of his total and unshakable love for each of us. Along with this comes our recognition of his love for everyone else. He loves the old gentle Jewish man whose teeth are wrenched out of his mouth for the gold fillings. And, Jesus loves the S. S. officer who pulls those teeth out. Jesus' love for each of them causes him to experience indescribable agony. This becomes clearer to us the more *we look out with him from the Cross. We pray as he prays.* Jesus' *outlook* becomes ours. We see the world around us with his intensity. This is an awesome and *terrible* experience."

Edith's friend Maximilian Kolbe, who died in the Auschwitz concentration camp, spoke.

"Yes friends, we are now able to penetrate the *deeper* meaning of the verse; "It is a *terrible thing* to fall into the hands of the living God." (Hebrews 10:31) It is *terrible and awesome* to fall into the embrace of Jesus' nailed hands. Jesus' hands, God's hands, are *nailed in love* to every human being. All the powers of hell cannot shake God from the nailed position of love that Jesus has established. This is the fixed stance of the Blessed Trinity's eternal love for each of us. When I look out from the Cross, accepting and feeling the warmth of God's love for me, my prayer for myself and everyone else, becomes increasingly enthusiastic and joyful."

A young woman was the next to speak. It was France's Jeanne d'Arc. Most of us know her by the English version of her name, Joan of Arc.

"We pray best when we agree with God's estimation that we are worth nurturing and even dying for. We have to stop putting ourselves down. To keep praying in sync with God we will need to revise some of the prayers handed on to us."

Jesus walked over to Joan. "You are so right, *ma chère* Jeanne. Here is one example of a prayer that needs changing. This prayer is taken from a hymn often used in the Divine Office.

MAXIMILIAN KOLBE (1894 – 1941) is one of ten 20th-century martyrs who are depicted in statues above the Great West Door of Westminster Abbey, London.

He was a Polish Franciscan friar who volunteered to die in place of another man in the Nazi concentration camp of Auschwitz in Poland. He was canonized by Pope John Paul II on 10 October, 1982, in the presence of Franciszek Gajowniczek whose life he saved.

JOAN OF ARC or Jeanne d'Arc in French (c. 1412 – 1431) was a 15th century saint and national heroine of France. She was tried and executed by the English for witchcraft when she was only 19 years old. Earlier she had been found guilty of heresy by the Catholic Church in France. Twenty-four years after being burned at the stake, the Vatican reviewed the French decision and she was found innocent and declared a martyr. She was canonized a saint in 1920.

Eternal Father, loving God,
Who made us from the dust of earth,
Transform us by the Spirit's grace,
Give value to our little *worth.*

"I would prefer the last line of the hymn to say: 'Give value to our GREAT worth and thus conform to *my* outlook from the Cross.'"

Blessed Isaac of Stella waited for Jesus to sit down.

Then he rose to share his thoughts with the group. They all knew that there was a website dedicated to Isaac of Stella's writings. They were anxious to hear what he had to say about prayer. He spoke. "*Feeling* God's eternal and unchangeable

ISAAC OF STELLA: (c. 1100 – 1169) He was born in England and died in France. He was a monk, theologian and philosopher. He joined the Order of Cistercians, during the reforms of Saint Bernard of Clairvaux. Iaaac's writings are still revered.

love for us makes prayer *comfortable* and *nurturing.* In order to preserve this contented and happy acceptance of God's love for us, Jesus fires a warning shot across our bow."

Jesus interrupted him. "What do you mean Izaac?"

"Remember Lord how you warned people, 'Don't join the party of the Pharisees. Don't give in an inch to them.' You were anxious to make us wary of any voice that would diminish our confidence in God's embrace of us."

Jesus stood up. "Isaac is correct, people. All of you know that I loved each Pharisee. Why then did I come down so hard on them? It's because of the energy they put into condemning, excluding and ostracizing anyone that they perceived not to their liking. They had forgotten what *God* likes, what God loves and what God *wants.* You all *know what God wants*: Every person's *completion and wholeness.* God's love rejects *all* pharisaical exclusion, *all* apartheid."

Jesus sat down.

His mother, Mary, rose. "God wants to remove whatever prevents any of us finding our own inner goodness. God wants to help people recognize their *huge value* and become *fully free, fully human, fully themselves."*

"Thank you Mother," Jesus said: "That is the view of prayer from the Cross." Then Jesus turned to Izaac of Stella: "Isaac do you have anything else you would like to say about prayer?"

"Yes Lord, thank you; I do. I feel the need to emphasize praying that you, your Father and your Spirit free us from the blindness of an unfortunately common *un*belief; not believing that *every* human person is precious; every US citizen, every Iraqi, every Palestinian, every Jew, every Muslim. The value of each member of the human family is universal. Anything less than accepting the worth of every human being is unbelief and blind and *prevents us praying at all.*

"Thank you Isaac." Jesus rose to speak again. "I am particularly concerned with how people use the prayer that I handed on to everybody known as the

Lord's Prayer, the *Our Father.* It is unfortunate when the phrase 'Your will be done' is interpreted to mean 'Your will be done, as *I understand it!*' People need to pray the Our Father as *I, Jesus, understand it* from my view from the Cross. 'Our Father, hallowed be your name.' That means, hallowed be your love for Tom and Sally, hallowed be your love for Dick and Jane, hallowed by your love for Harry and Joanne. When anyone attempts to pray the Lord's Prayer and does *not* honor, hallow, and reverence my Father's love for Tom, Dick and Harry, the words in their prayer are no longer *hallow* — become *hollow*."

Mary, Jesus' mother, rose again to speak. "Son, as long as we are considering revising some prayers, I would prefer it if people made a change in the *Ave Maria*. They say 'Pray for us sinners now and at the hour of our death.' I would prefer them to say, 'Pray for us *children,* now and at the hour of our death.' There is no research grant needed to delve into the question: do people sin? Or; can human beings do awful stuff? They can. But you, my son Jesus, have come to turn the tide, no matter what the gravitational pull—turn the tide of each person's life away from sin and towards being fully human and able to share divine life with you. What a difference if people remembered they were children — *God's children."*

Joseph, Mary's husband and Jesus' foster father on Earth, rose to share his thoughts. "I took care of you, Jesus, all those years when you were a child and teenager. I know how people can really come close to you in prayer. They must *never* exclude *anyone* from their love. When they seek *communion* with you in prayer, they need to identify with your feelings for the homeless person, for the scared convict on Death Row, for the drug user or drug dealer. I pray that theirs is always a *Holy Communion."*

17

Holy Communion

THOMAS AQUINAS RETURNED to spend more time looking out with Jesus from Calvary. Hundreds of years ago, Thomas wrote about the Eucharist, and what it meant to receive Holy Communion. He spoke to everyone on the Hill. "The more *whole* and therefore *holy* our communions with Jesus are, the more we become enthused with helping others to attain their calling, to be true to themselves. The growth of the human family does *not* depend on *how many* churchgoers partake of the Sacrament. Rather, it is the number of worshippers whose communion with Jesus has *converted them to his view from the Cross*. They stand beside the risen Christ. They stay entrenched on the hill where he established the dominion of divine love. They are able to look out with him from Calvary, with uncomplicated and unselective love for every person.

"So, everyone: when is it a *Holy* Communion? The communion is holy when the person coming to the altar is willing to receive all whom Jesus loves.

If anyone excludes *one* person from her or his love, then that communion *loses its holiness*. The fruit of *Holy* Communion is the knowledge that there is no space between hatred and love. We always choose one or the other. How many people do we receive in Holy Communion? Do we receive as many as Jesus receives? Our communion is as *holy* as the number of people we are willing to receive into our hearts. *Any* anti-*one* human person — *any* rejection — and there is no *holy* communion."

Jesus smiled and said: "Thank you Thomas. You have clearly and succinctly taught everyone what is needed for Communion with me to be *Holy.*" He paused and then spoke slowly and deliberately. "Your communion with me is most likely to be *holy* when you abandon the heresy of certainty: yes!—*the heresy of certainty.*

18

Certainty

DOROTHY DAY (1897–1980): She founded the Catholic Worker movement to care for the poorest of the poor and to promote peace throughout the whole world.

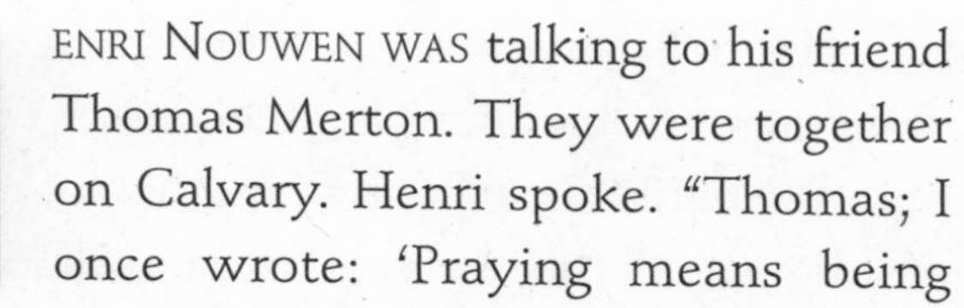

HENRI NOUWEN WAS talking to his friend Thomas Merton. They were together on Calvary. Henri spoke. "Thomas; I once wrote: 'Praying means being constantly ready to let go of your certainty and move on further than where you now are.'"

Merton answered. "I agree Henri. Jesus, from the Cross, is telling us not to bother being certain and correct all of the time. He is saying to us: 'Even with all the pain and confusion that can get mixed in with the joy of life, if you stay looking out from here with me you'll be certain of this. You are loved and you will always be loved. You'll come out, like Alice, just fine at the other end.' "

Dorothy Day was with them.

She spoke. "*Knowing* one is *loved:* Isn't that heaps better than being *always* certain? Hitler and Stalin seemed so far apart and yet they had in common their *certainty.* Mussolini, early in his career shared their certainty and committed horrible atrocities in Ethiopia. Later in his life he became less certain and so he did a bit less damage."

Henri Nouwen said. "Dorothy, *their* certainty was dogmatic and hard as steel. Jesus' certainty was not dogmatic. That's obvious in Gethsemane. He didn't have all the answers for himself. So he prayed for answers. And he got them. They were painful. Eventually he rose to indestructible life from facing up to those tough answers."

Thomas Merton nodded. "Yes, like all of us at times, Jesus *wrestled* with uncertainty and the temptation to lose heart. He wavered. Maybe he wanted to give up? But, he didn't. Like the great Jewish patriarch Jacob, Jesus struggled with doubts and fear but did not give in to despair. Why didn't he? What got him up onto his feet in the Garden of Gethsemane? It was because he *felt* certain of his Father's love.

Caryll Houselander was with them.

She felt it time for her to contribute to the conversation. "Yes. Jesus felt it. He lost interest in being 100% certain. He probably had it as a child. However, by the time he invited himself into the house of the tax collector Zacchaeus, Jesus made

CARYLL HOUSELANDER (b. 1901, d. 1954), a woodcarver and church artist by trade, was an influential and popular Catholic writer.

decisions based on his *feelings*. He trusted his own feelings. Fantastic. He knew he was on much surer ground than relying on being certain. Feelings: without them there is no *room* for *being*: only room for being certain."

Dorothy Day spoke again. "People like Francis of Assisi and Joan of Arc were emptied of holding tightly to the illusion of individual dogmatic certainty. They knew where they stood. They knew, as Jesus knows from his risen and indestructible view *from* the cross, that they were loved. Aren't we caught up in a confrontation of certainty? September 11, 2001 revealed how catastrophic is the certainty of dogmatism. The escalation of conflict since then shows us the consequences that threaten our human family when certainty confronts certainty. The certainty of dogma is clung to and one group flexes its muscles and another responds. Each of them, espousing a different set of dogmas of certainty, rush headlong into unthinkable horror."

"I agree," Thomas Merton said. "This feeling of being 100% correct was what prompted religious and political zealots to arrange Jesus' crucifixion. For followers of Jesus, there is the same danger of preaching from dogmatic certainty rather than *from his Cross.*"

They all looked up to see Jesus coming to join them. He spoke. "I'm glad you are talking about the danger of certainty. Dogmatic certainty can block out so much love. Being 100% sure — how narrow become all the horizons in every direction. I died without a trace of competing for dogmatic certainty. I had reached *the absolute assuredness of knowing I was loved.* So I said simply: 'Father, into your hands I commend my spirit.' *From* the cross, I'm saying to all preachers, clerics, ecclesiastics, rabbis, mullahs, and every possible sort of guru: 'Let me show you how you can help people. Tell them that they'll be able to see *from* my viewpoint here, from my cross, that none of them needs dogmatic certainty. I didn't need it myself. What I needed, I had. I needed to know my Father's love. Tell people that if they practice with me, looking out *from* my Cross, I'll gently bring them into the depth of that *feeling* of how much my Father loves them.'

None of them spoke for a few moments. Then Thomas Merton spoke again. "Lord, thank you for what you just said about the danger of certainty. After falling into the chasm of dogmatic certainty, it can be so difficult to emerge. The anthropologist can trip and fall into the pit of certainty by *dismissing* the concept of creation and creator. This can happen because of the amazing dogmatism in asserting 'my explanation of the origin of species is complete and certain. There is no need for any further discussion!' The theologian can stumble into a similar bottomless well of dogmatic certainty by denying every tenet of evolution."

Jesus said. "Yes Thomas, now that I have risen

from the experience of sharing in *all* the world's pain, I look out over this planet and think: 'Father, if only they weren't so certain!' "

Peter had joined them and made a confession. "Hullo everyone:" Then he turned to Jesus. "I thought that I knew what was best for you Lord. *I* was handicapped by a form of dogmatic certainty. I tried to dissuade you from going to Jerusalem and so avoid the Cross. I laid a terrible temptation in front of you; it was the temptation to avoid confrontation even if it meant denying one's own self. And you Lord, in *no uncertain* way, told me to back off."

Jesus smiled. "Yes, Peter; people live in a world awash with dogmatic certainty. This flood of crippling arrogance is threatening to stifle humanity from Kabul to Tel Aviv, from Belfast to Rome."

Jesus then turned to everyone on the Hill with him: "You all know the expression 'the truth shall make you free'. The truth that frees people is the knowledge that each of them doesn't need dogmatism when they can experience the *feeling* of being *certain that they are loved.*"

Epilogue

SAINT PAUL WRITES in his Second Letter to the Corinthians: 1:22:

"It is God who gives both us and you our certainty in Christ." Jesus went to Calvary to show us what is certain: that we are loved, that we are of inestimable value. It is the

best location to look out from. The view is stunning. We can return there and invite whoever we like to share the view with us. There is no distortion. There is no smog; just a clear vision opened up before us by someone who knows us really well.

Jesus has something of everybody in himself. He can relate to the experience of each person. Jesus has his feminine side and masculine side. He has his liberal bent and his conservative inclination. He was the traditionalist in lots of ways and still the innovator like no other. He believed and still believes in you and me. He loves us — how he loves us. His destiny is ours; freedom, fullness, completion. Right now we are in a process of becoming: every day we continue on the journey to being fully ourselves. It will help us to participate in their conversations and share with Jesus and his friends our *Views from the Cross.*

Permissions

Page 65: *Jerusalem Bible*, Copyright 1966, 1967, 1968: Darton, Longman & Todd and Doubleday & Co, Inc.

Page 66: Hart, Thomas, N. *The Art of Christian Living*, published by Paulist Press, New York/Mahwah, New Jersey, 1980, Used with permission. www.paulistpress.com.

Page 128: Psalm 26:8, Psalm 28:2b, Psalm 134: 1b, 2a: Copyright © 1963, *The Grail*, England. GIA Publications, Inc., exclusive North American agent. All rights reserved. Used by permission.

Page 139: Hymn, *Eternal Father, Living God, Stanbrook Abbey Hymnal*: Copyright Benedictine Nuns of Stanbrook Abbey, Wass, York, England, UK.

Page 151: Excerpted from *With Open Hands,* Henri J. M. Nouwen. Copyright ©1972, 1995, 2005 by Ave Maria Press, P.O. Box 428, Notre Dame, IN 46556, www.avemaria-press.com. Used with permission of the publisher.

Page 157: Epilogue: Second Corinthians 1: 21,22: Knox translation of the Bible, Second Edition, 1956: used with permission: Continuum International Publishing Group.

Sincere apologies are extended if there are other acknowledgments inadvertently omitted that should have been included.